RATIONAL RECOVERY MASTERY

Starter Kit

No part of this publication can be replicated or distributed in any form without the written permission of the author or publisher.

Louis D. Gonzales-Ph.D., CMLC

Minneapolis, Minnesota
www.startingpointacademy.com
(612) 483-767

WELCOME TO STARTING POINT ACADEMY

Who am I to be conducting this training? I am not a therapist. I don't *treat* anyone. I am a life strategist; an aftercare recovery coach who has been professionally educated and trained in behavioral theory and has been coaching others for success for over 25 years. The clients I work with choose my services, sometimes as an addition to their aftercare program. They are highly motivated and want additional support and accountability to help them achieve their goal of a healthier lifestyle after treatment. My job is to listen, and to ask the right question. Everyone in life utilizes a coach at some point be it a tennis coach, diabetic coach, and those struggling with life's transitions. Why not coaches for persons with addictive disorders?

In the past, I have coached, explained, pushed, pulled, and coaxed young people in their time of despair. In my Doctorate work in *Continued Community Care* I knew that at those times especially, there was a great need for a voice of common sense that could stand by them and provide them with direction.

It wasn't called recovery coaching then, but today, I know that's what it was. I still am of the belief that deep and powerful change is possible. Can you imagine working with someone when both of you are on the same heartbeat? I have experienced this and now I will help you do it too. I am moved by what I do and I will never stop doing it. Welcome aboard!

Member and Affiliate of:

Starting Point Academy: Trainer of Trainers

Fowler International Academy of Professional Coaching

Recovery Coach Network

Recovery Coach International

National Association of Alcoholism and Drug Abuse Counselors (NAADAC)

National Association of Anger Management.

Using Your Starter Kit

➢ This is your Starter Kit. It is meant to be written in, doodled in, personalized, dog-eared, spilled on, and protected. So please write your name on the inside cover so that if you lose it you'll get it back.

➢ At the conclusion of each module (1-10) there is a place in this journal to write any inquires you might have in the future and a place to response to two questions:

1) *What insights about coaching did you gain out of that particular module?*

2) *How will what you learned be applied to your work as a Recovery Coach?*

➢ Every aspect of coaching is about building relationships. It is a human condition that we first make decisions based on feelings or emotional reasoning; and second through rational thinking. The dilemma becomes one of clients being mired in emotional decision-making resulting in erroneous thinking habits that get them into trouble.

Keep your coaching work on a positive context:

- ➢ Be here now, prepared. Be somewhere else later.
- ➢ Reality can be changed with thoughtful and rational discussion.
- ➢ Always invite the truth from your clients.
- ➢ Rely on your instincts. (where is this person taking me?)
- ➢ Explore options that lead to healthier decisions.
- ➢ Work collaboratively with clients.
- ➢ Like a Texan oil man, drill deeper until you strike oil.
- ➢ Remain respectfully curious at all times *(Hmm. Tell me more?")*
- ➢ When at an impasse, wait it out. It pays to let silence do the heavy lifting.
- ➢ Interrogate reality, not clients.
- ➢ Use cost-benefit analysis to help clients arrive at an impetus for change.
- ➢ Check for incongruence.
- ➢ Engage in a mutually enthusiastic relationship.

YOU AS COACH

Professional and personal traits can vary from coach to coach. There are some common qualities inherent in all coaches that play a critical role in affecting the bond that is created between coach and client that allows for self-awareness to occur.

You are already a curious individual; an empathetic listener and a *connector* of people to professional and resources in your community. As a general rule, you tend to bring the following qualities to the coaching process:

- ✓ Naturally curious about people and the world around you.
- ✓ Already working/volunteering in a helping capacity (A.A. Sponsor; peer coaching, clinician; etc.)
- ✓ Emotionally balanced.
- ✓ Curious about the world around you.
- ✓ Believes there are several paths to wellness.
- ✓ More spatial than linear in problem-solving.
- ✓ Easily provides sincere encouragement.
- ✓ Gets a joy out of helping others.
- ✓ Open to trying different personal/professional approaches.
- ✓ Out-of-the-box thinker.

✓ Active and empathetic listener.
✓ Creative and open-minded.
✓ High level of energy.
✓ A good sense of reality and humor (it is what it is).
✓ Open-minded regarding spirituality, alternate lifestyles and general understanding of different cultures.
✓

What did we leave out?

1. ____
2. ____
3. ____
4. ____
5. ____

ADDICTION: IT'S NOT WHAT YOU THINK

Addiction is not necessarily a brain disease, but more of a *disconnection* disorder a disease of loneliness. There, I said it. Addiction is a result of a *disconnection* from the five universal life elements which when missing or ignored can results in behaviors that lead to addiction. They include the: *Physical, mental, emotional, social,* and *spiritual.*

Most humans need a social and spiritual connection in order to survive. It's our nature. Anyone who cannot find a purpose or connection to anyone or anything in the universe can easily become crushed by the weight of isolation and disconnection, resulting in forming bonds and a dependency on anything addictive, legal or not, that can fill their void or emptiness. These are the underlying factors of addiction. In our work with recovering clients we have seen a link between a reduced capacity to *connect* with human or spiritual connections and the increased risk of drug or antisocial behavior dependency

 **CHANGING ADDICTIVE THINKING**

Fighting addictions and other compulsive behaviors is a challenge. Alcoholics, addicts and persons with compulsive behaviors should use all the available tools at their disposal to overcome their challenges.

Thoughts are powerful, and they do shape a person's life. This is because the way that people think impacts the way they experience the world. When addicted individuals become trapped in addictive thinking, it will determine much of how they will perceive the world. Now in recovery, their addictive thinking habits from the past still linger and continue to be influenced by past alcohol and drugs defenses known as *cognitive distortions*. That is all addicts have known all their addicted lives. Your job is to help clients break through these self-deceptive habits.

ABOUT RECOVERY

➢ Emerges from hope: Sends message of a better future.

➢ Person driven: self determined and self-directed (you gotta want it bad!)

➢ Occurs via many pathways: People have distinct needs, preferences, and cultural backgrounds.

➢ Is holistic: encompasses whole life that includes physical, emotional, intellectual, social, and spiritual domains.

➢ Supported by peers and allies. All individuals play a support and cross-accountability role in recovery.

➢ Personal strengths-based: Taps into a client's inner strengths.

➢ Solutions-focused: through collaborative relationship, clients learn to be their own rescuers.

What is Recovery Coaching

Recovery coaching is a person-centered, strengths-based system that upholds the notion that there can be several paths to sobriety. Recovery coaching is highly interactive in that the client is encouraged to actively participate in their own recovery. The coaching process is action oriented with an emphasis on improving present life and reaching goals for the future. It is based on the belief that people by their very nature are creative, resourceful and whole.

Recovery Coaching *is* about:

Guiding optimism

Open acceptance

Strengths-focused

Non-linear thinking

Client-centered

Empowering

Interactive

Growth-focused

Understanding of spiritual concepts

Clients set the agenda

Empathetic and knowledgeable partner

Challenges the problem not the client.

Recovery Coaching is *NOT* about:

Top-down interaction	Shaming
Advising	Linear thinking
Confrontive	Excavating past traumas
Labeling problems	"Do it our way," mentality
Minimizing problems	Angering clients
Challenging clients	diagnosing
Psycho-babbling to impress	Addressing past issues

THE RECOVERY COACH

- Recovery coaches are non-clinical professionals who help people strategize, plan and make positive changes in their lives. They don't diagnose or treat addiction or other mental health issues. Recovery coaches only work with people experiencing transitional challenges related to addictive substances or compulsive behaviors, and in need of continued aftercare help. Recovery coaching is not a one-size-fits-all paradigm and maintains that there are several paths to recovery beyond sitting in a circle, hugging a box of Kleenex and (though helpful) memorizing steps.

- Recovery coaching is about "growth" not rescue. A Recovery Coach uses a present-future action-oriented approach by asking probing or focused questions that empowers clients to achieve clarity and the motivation for making decisions and plans that will improve their lives, one step at a time. Coaches don't dabble in past traumas, and only support forward-moving positive change.

As a recovery coach, you are about growth, not rescue. You will allow your clients the flexibility of exploring multiple paths and options while on their sober journey. Your task will be to guide and support them in their selection of options and to help them devise a plan to make their chosen options a reality. Our training system emphasizes the fact that there can be several paths to sobriety and you will be helping clients explore this tenet through field-tested uses of empirical evidence, logic, and a process known as cognitive restructuring: a realignment of one's faulty thinking and beliefs. You will maintain a professional, but collaborative relationship that will focus on trust, support, and mutual accountability. Your goal will be to help a client achieve a life they once dearly loved, but was lost through addictive or compulsive behaviors.

NEGATIVE INTERNAL DIALOGUE

Clients will also tend to engage in an excessive amount of negative (addictive) thinking, known as *"internal dialogue"* or *self-talk* will use this to justify their behavior. Individuals in recovery who hope to break away from addictive habits need to change the way they think or will either relapse or continue living in an alternative reality made up of self-deceptions.

Many humans go about their daily lives having a running commentary going on in their heads. This internal voice is constantly interpreting things and making judgments and decisions. It can act as the individual's biggest cheerleader or their harshest critic. This commentary inside the person's head creates the "lens" by which the person perceives the world and interacts with it. It is created through a combination of conscious thought and unconscious beliefs (past programming). Starting Point Academy refers to negative self-talk as having *"cognitive distortions."* (aka: stinky thinking).

 **DISTORTED THINKING HABITS**

Negative self-talk or *distorted thinking* is known as your *inner critic* and can often be brought into the coaching setting resulting in active interaction or conflict. This negative internal monologue can seriously interfere with one's ability to self-access and move forward in one's recovery. Female addicts in recovery refer to distorted thinking as their *"inner bitch."*

A negative internal monologue can sabotage a person's recovery and comes in different varieties such as:

- Pessimism about the future.
- Bitterness about the past.
- Overly critical of own behavior.
- Resenting other people.
- Finding reasons to criticize any progress.
- An unwillingness to forgive themselves for past mistakes.
- Having unreasonable expectations for themselves.
- Blowing things out of proportion

- Negative self-fulfilling prophecy. By thinking negatively the individual can cause negative things to happen to them.
- Reduced self-efficacy. Individual doubt their own ability to achieve a task.
- Suffer from anxiety. Persistent internal monologue makes the world feel like a threatening place.
- Distorted thinking can lead to symptoms of depression.
- Stinky thinking can prevent the individual from achieving their goals in sobriety.
- Negative dialoguing reduces any motivation so that the individual feels unable to do the things they need to do to build a successful sobriety.
- It means that when the person does something good or achieves success they will not be able to fully enjoy their victory. Their "inner bitch" will always find something to complain about.
- It will often be this negative self talk or inner bitch that drove the individual to abuse alcohol or drugs in the first place. If they continue with this type of thinking in recovery they will likely turn to other maladaptive behaviors in order to cope.
- Negative self-talk or what we call *"self-flagellation"* creates a negative self-fulfilling prophesy

In short, negative self-talk create a negative *self fulfilling prophecy*; making a negative prediction a reality.   Not only that, but persistent negative distorted thinking not only creates failure, but it also provides the perfect excuse for relapse. At the very least, it can cause the individual to suffer from severe anxiety. This negative internal monologue means that the world can feel like a threatening place.

Whatcha Gonna Do?

Be aware of client resistance. Resistance is a way clients protect themselves from painful experiences. A prudent coach needs to begin working on a client's resistance gradually. It's okay to interrupt when coaching in order to get more clarity when challenging resistance. *(wait, help me understand...")* Don't talk about *change* at first. Clients go into convulsions when faced with notion of having to make a change. Instead refer to coaching as making small adjustments. In time, those small adjustments will become the change the client is searching for. The 4E process outlined in the next page   is very helpful in building trust and confidence when coaching a resistant client.

The **4E** process:

Engage clients to comfortably express their concerns.

Encourage clients to reach out and take a few risks.

Empower clients to begin exploring options and setting small goals and adjustments.

Evaluate not only client's progress, but your own as well.

Let go of your agenda. This is not about you. Let the client do the driving and just ask simple question to see where they lead. Also, avoid playing therapist. Do not diagnose or label the client's state of mind. Instead, just ask, *"Interesting. Tell me more."* One last point; speak in a language the client understands. The use of metaphors and analogies can be very helpful in recovery coaching.

WHOLE LIFE RECOVERY

"Reconnection is the antidote to relapsing"

Starting Point has incorporated Whole Life Recovery (WLR) in its work with clients. It is the cornerstone of reconnecting oneself to a successful recovery and life. If *disconnection* from life's rewards is the road leading to addiction, then *reconnection* must be the road back. Addicted or not, there exist five life elements which are critical to living a well-balanced and healthy life and includes the: ***physical, mental, emotional, social and spiritual*** aspects of wellness that in recovery must be kept in balance if we are to experience a lasting, healthy lifestyle.

Whole Life Recovery as used in recovery coaching takes from both Buddhist thought and Native American teachings which emphasize five life domains that include the physical, emotional, mental, social and spiritual aspects of wellness that work in unison and when kept in balance, we can experience a balanced and healthy life. The combination of the five life domains or elements work together to revitalize and balance the body which in turn provides us with contentment, fulfillment, a sense of wholeness, wellness and happiness.

HOW WHOLE LIFE RECOVERY WORKS

The Whole Life Recovery paradigm encourages clients to begin exploring options that can address all five life elements, and as much as possible include each life element in a client's personal recovery plan. This is known in coaching as *"building recovery capital."* Whole Life Recovery (WLR) takes a positive view of its clients and offers them the opportunity to explore alternative sets of habits and beliefs and store them in each life element in order to tap into any one of them when needed. People who exhibit these five life elements are referred to as *whole* beings…and isn't being *whole* a goal of recovery?

Full recovery is not just about staying off addictive substances or behaviors. It is about building up enough *recovery capital* in all five life domains and maintaining those strengths to make positive lifestyle changes. It becomes critical that the recovery coach introduce this concept in a manner that clients can easily understand.

WHOLE LIFE RECOVERY
A TEACHING MODEL

I have found real-life analogies useful when explaining concepts that may seem murky or too sophisticated for clients to understand. A good example is a teaching model that relates to recovery capital and asks clients to imagine for a moment that our body is like an automobile with four tires and a steering wheel. The tires and the steering wheel represent five universal life domains needed to guide us on life's journey; in this case, sobriety.

| Physical | Mental | Emotional | Social | Spiritual |

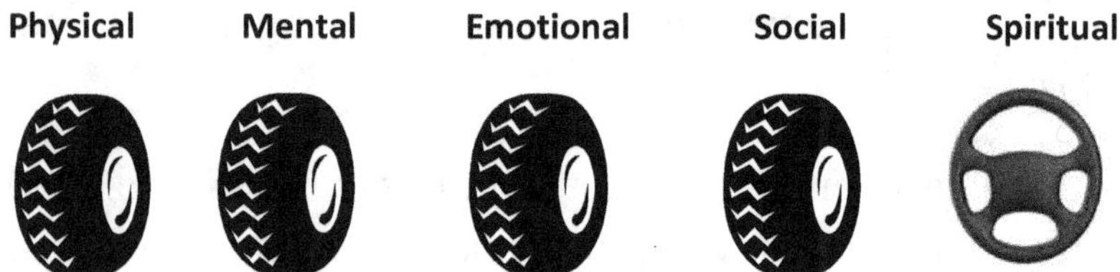

Recovery is about applying a *whole life* perspective to living a wholesome lifestyle and it happens through the reconnection with five universal life domains that, once helped us feel balanced, made it easier for us to face each new day with purpose. We refer to it as *Whole Life Recovery.* There's data surfacing that supports my assertion, that a *reconnection* to supernatural rewards such as good health, sharp mind, balance emotions, supportive relationships, and a solid spiritual-base is a core part of any recovery. If *disconnection* is the precursor to addiction, then *reconnection* must be the antidote.

RECOVERY CAPITAL

The five life domains mentioned above work synergistically to revitalize and balance the mind, body, and spirit while maintaining a balanced and fulfilled life. We must do all the hard work by monitoring and ensuring that each life domain has its sufficient complement of *recovery capital* needed to draw upon when times get tough; and they will. Recovery Capital is defined as: *having enough resources that are necessary to begin and stay in recovery from addiction, alcoholism, or any legal compulsive disorder.*

Here's my argument. If there is any validity in my *disconnection-reconnection* theory relating to the five life domains, then maybe we need to begin calling any compulsive disorder, addiction being one, a *lack of relationship disease* and a *reconnection* to those five mentioned life domains as the antidote.

Whole Life Recovery teaches that a reconnection to life's five domains can bring a person back to balance and forms the foundation for a sound recovery. One life domain cannot be excluded from the other. It means building recovery capital in each and making substantial adjustments to our whole pattern of living; a life-style make-over. In doing so, the five life elements come together as one force in the universe that can support our efforts in learning to live life all over again.

RECOVERY CAPITAL PLAN

Human and recovery capital are used interchangeably and are an essential commodity throughout life's journey. Each of us has the potential to give and receive and store human-recovery capital when needed.

Physical Domain - Get thee to a gym. When you are feeling stressed, anxious, or depressed, exercise is often the last thing you will think of, but that is probably the time when your brain needs it the most. Our task in recovery is put ourselves through a process of exploring ways of building recovery capital in the physical domain by taking back our good health and maintaining stability through physical care. Begin to bike, swim, lift weights, do yoga...whatever it takes. But don't burn yourself out trying to do everything at once. Avoid exhaustion and get enough rest.

Mental Domain - Begin by challenging your distorted thinking patterns and beliefs, and begin making reality checks: "Who owns this problem anyway?" "Says who..." until challenging and fact-checking becomes an in-grained habit and your "go-to" place for reality-checking... Don't get yourself in self-defeating, limiting mind trips. Avoid rationalizing or minimizing your recovery journey. Learn ways to stimulate yourself intellectually. Read up on recovery. Take a class at the local college;

tutor kids; volunteer. Just don't let yourself get bored. Remember that boredom and relapse are close cousins. Stay mentally active. Your task here is to begin cleaning out your metaphorical closet. You will begin to notice that as your mind becomes clearer, you will become stronger and better able to understand that your former addiction cannot define who you are as an individual.

Emotional Domain - When troubled or unsure as to how your recovery is going, ask for help. As you evolve, you begin to store up "recovery capital" that will strengthen and transform you as you become better able to forgive yourself and begin asking those you hurt for forgiveness. Don't bottle up your feelings by letting them build up inside you. Join a support group. Use it to express your feelings and emotions and do some fact-checking.

Social Domain - Face it. We are all social beings, with a strong need to belong (modest example: cell phone and social media addiction).

No one ever recovers alone. People in recovery need people. Recovery is about adopting a culture of new shared values that are positive, support sobriety, and enhances well-being. Socialization through A.A., N.A. recovery coaching support groups, SMART Recovery and other fellowships play an invaluable role in addiction recovery. Persons in recovery encourage and engage with each other. They provide each other with the support needed to recover and, more importantly, to maintain that recovery. Studies have shown that persons involved in any type of social fellowship often benefit from improved social functioning, family adjustments.

Spiritual Domain - You are entitled to happiness and the joy that sobriety brings. It is now time to begin risking a little and discover your inner path. It doesn't have to be a religious experience, but if it is, so much the better. Spirituality in recovery is more about discovering the power of gratitude that changes self-pity into a new-found peace. It is about regaining or rebuilding your moral character once again through the practice of humility, tolerance, forgiveness, responsibility, and concern for others. This is a good time to begin building recovery capital for the challenging times ahead. Begin by not looking behind or ahead. Instead, look up in gratitude for where you are now. There is no greater time than in recovery where you will need the support and guidance of God...your Higher Power.

"But isn't that practicing religion," you ask? No, but we often unconsciously link the two. It is helpful at this final point to separate spirituality and religion. Spirituality does not need to be defined through the lens of religion. Religion can be thought of as a set of beliefs, rituals, rules and protocols regarding a belief or deity. Spirituality is a personal search for meaning in life through prayer or meditation while maintaining a connection with God and all things powerful in the universe.

 **What Happens If We Get A Flat Tire?**

Keeping with the aforementioned analogy, getting a flat tire (relapsing) is not the end of our sober journey. Every relapse episode can be traced back to a neglect of one or more of the five life elements. Gone unchecked, the effects of neglect can be multi-dimensional and can take its toll on all five life elements. Setbacks are going to happen, can be used as learning experiences and a time for practicing new skills; not something to retreat from and be ashamed. Setbacks are viewed as opportunities for clients to analyze and understand what went wrong and how things might be handled better the next time a setback occurs.

What about the steering wheel analogy? I dabbled in "Religious Studies" while in college and have learned that the metaphorical steering mechanism may just be the most important life element in our recovery journey. The steering wheel serves as our guide that helps us navigate away from trouble and sets us back in a right direction. But the thing that gets in our way of a well-balanced life is *arrogance*. We think we can solve all challenges by ourselves, and refer to prayer and meditation only as a last resort. We never give thanks when the sun shines, but only when it storms.

INTENTIONAL INQUIRY

What Motivates Clients to Change?

The basis of recovery coaching is founded on the principle that clients are the experts on themselves.   That said, here's what I've discovered in my own work:

1) Clients are motivated to change *only* if they think that the change will benefit them. Coaches need to concentrate in guiding clients in developing realistic, measurable, and achievable goals and action plans. Otherwise clients will set aside those goals in the "too hard" bin of their mental closet.

2) Clients will *not* consider adopting new behaviors if the old behaviors (good or bad) are still working for them.

3) Clients are *more willing* to consider new or alternative behaviors if the alternative behaviors are <u>equally</u> or <u>more</u> beneficial than the original behaviors. The client may find yoga or exercising more relaxing than drinking, for example.

4) Clients need to be *convinced* of their own ability to change. Coaches do what they can to support client self-confidence faith in themselves.

Whatcha Gonna Do?

➢ Maintain an interactive, but inquisitive, conversational style of coaching and a key component in the change process.

➢ Practice asking *"Sez who?"* or *"So what."* It helps clients connect the dots and what it means to the larger picture.

➢ It's okay to respectfully interrupt*: "Wait, wait. Help me understand your view point."*

➢ Drill deeply with solutions-focused questioning. It is a good way of getting buy-in and empowering clients to open up in more honest ways.

➢ Using goal-oriented questions, the coach is sending a message that says, *"You are the main player in this change process (not me) and you are the one that has to decide.* When this becomes your mantra, it will invite your clients to risk a bit more and empower them to do things they thought they would never be capable of doing which is moving closer to taking responsibility for their own change.

ADDRESSING LEARNED HELPLESSNESS

Clients are looking for answers to the questions they already know the answers to. In coaching we call it *"learned helplessness."* That's all many clients know. They have spent an inordinate amount of time being blamed, shamed, and told what they ought to do and not do. Many have never been encouraged to take action on their own behalf and or have tried to become their own rescuers. While cocooned in a treatment setting, clients may have learned a few basic relapse prevention or recovery skills, but are now out in the real world, where the risks have quadrupled, and are suddenly feeling intimidated by the standards and challenges of the sober world. Giving answers and advice to clients is never a good thing. Instead, ask.

ASKING HAS POWER

One important role of recovery is the chemistry between the coach and client. Curiously asking questions presented in a conversational format, quickly defines the relationship. When coaches advise, they now become the "experts" and take on a role of intellectual superiority over their clients, at least in knowledge. But when a coach supports clients in challenging their maladaptive thinking and beliefs, the coach is then viewed not so much as an expert, but as an authentic, empathetic, and knowledgeable partner. This form of solutions-focused questioning is known as *Intentional Interviewing*, a form of collaboratively exploring options and solutions. Asking creates buy-in; buy-in creates empowerment; and empowerment creates change-talk. With a little practice, it can be that simple.

GETTING STARTED

People in early recovery still carry with them residual, distorted beliefs about themselves and life. Everyone wants to be happy; that's a given especially with persons in recovery. But sometimes people in early recovery cling heavily to old distorted and useless thoughts and habits that get in the way of moving forward. Your job is to help clients break on through to the other side. What follows is a compilation of sample questions that will make you the "master" of questioning and will trigger change-talk and amazing self-change in your clients.

TOP FIVE MISTAKES COACHES MAKE

1) Asking closed questions: Simple 'yes' and 'no' answers can kill you.

2) Rambling Questioning: asking the same question different ways thus confusing the client. This is referred to as "shot-gunning" the client.

3) Refusing to interrupt when appropriate. You must manage the coaching process or your client will bird hop all over the place. Bring your client back into focus by interrupting when appropriate.

4) Rhetorical Questioning: This type of questioning could be interrupted by clients as biased, opinionated, emotional, and judgmental. *("What were you thinking?" "Isn't that a copout?")*

5) Asking *why* questions: *Why* questions makes clients shut down for protection from fear of exposure. *Why* questions cause clients to defend their position or justify their actions and place blame on others.

Whatcha Gonna do?

Practice this disclaimer at each introduction session:

I am a recovery coach or life strategist. I am not a therapist. I don't treat anyone. I am about growth...not rescue. Our mutual concern will be about solving your present condition and setting future goals that you can accomplish. I don't provide you with answers, but through the work we will do together, I will support you in your quest to find your own answers.

As your coach I will maintain a professional, but collaborative relationship that will focus on your strengths and abilities to conquer or cope with whatever is preventing you from meeting your goals or your dreams. Our relationship will be based on trust, logic, support, experience, and mutual accountability. My goals are to help you regain a life you once dearly loved, but was lost through your addictive or compulsive behaviors. This is what I am prepared to for you and you for yourself.

THE INITIAL INTERVIEW

It is important to articulate to a client from the beginning what recovery coaching is or is not and the role you will play in the coaching process. Approach the session from a point of respect for where the client is at.

"How's your day going?"

How did you feel driving here?

"What do you expect to gain from our coaching relationship?"
"Let me explain what 'Recovery Coaching' is all about."

Explain how your drug/alcohol use has interfered with family, school, or job.
"In a perfect world, what would you like to achieve?"

"What do you want to take from this session that can help you?"
"Why did you consider now to make a change in your life?"
"My role as coach is to take you where you are today and where you want to be tomorrow. We will not dwell too much on your past."

"What would be different in your life if you would…?"

CONVERSATION STARTERS

Always begin your session with a warm handshake as you introduce yourself. Work at clarifying client needs as most clients come to you unsure of what they really want or need. We call this phenomenon "self-limited" thinking and robs clients of the opportunity to begin thinking and setting creative goals for themselves. Always follow-up on client responses with, *"Interesting. Tell me more?"*

"How was your drive over here?"

"On a scale of 1-10 how are feeling right now?"

"I will help you find solutions or we will explore and create them together.

 "If you could do anything with your life starting today, what would that look like?"

"Interesting. Tell me more?""

"What do you do for a living?" What do you like best about your job?"

"What are some of the great things you have done in the past (or recently)?"

"What is the best thing about your life right now?

Setting the Agenda

Once you've discussed fees, procedures, etc you can begin setting the agenda whether it's a first or subsequent sessions.

"If your grandmother was looking down on you today what would she see?"

"What do you feel you would like to work on today?"

"What do you feel you need to focus on today?"

"Which action steps from last time do we need to follow up?"

"What challenges are you facing right now? Tell me more?"

"Is there anything from last week do we need to follow up further?"

"So, here's what I see happening this week…" (discussion) What are your feelings about going in that direction? "

"You will be given a small homework assignment at the end of each meeting which will be used as a discussion point for subsequent meetings. Does that sound okay?"

Challenging Client Motives

"How do you know if that's a true assessment?"

"You say you don't know. But if you did know, what would that look like.

"Okay, okay, then if what you're saying is true, then how come you…?"

"Says who…?"

"So, what made you conclude that…?"

"What led you to choose that option?"

"What tells you that is a realistic option?"

"What's keeping you from focusing on the road ahead?"

"Help me understand why it's okay to continue letting people …"

"You just mentioned that everyone is entitled to a little peace. Where did you hear that? What does peace mean to you and what would that look like if you had it?"

Disputing Beliefs- Barriers-Obstacles

"What do you think could be stopping you from…?"

"Sez who?"

"What part have you played in all this?"

"Explain that comment for me a bit more?"

"How will this problem manifest itself in the future if it is not solved?"

"What are some of the things you have already done to help you reach your goal?"

"How has that worked for you?

"You just said, "I don't know, but if you did know how would that look."

"What does that tell you?"

"Could you defend your position in a court of law?"

"So, what does that say about your position."

ALTERNATIVE ANALYSIS QUESTIONING

"What have you tried in the past to resolve this issue?"

"What was helpful? What was not helpful?

"What seemed to make things worse?"

"What seemed to make things better?"

"What if you were to consider trying…?"

"What would be the worst that could happen if you tried…?"

"What do mean by damned if you do and damned if you don't?"

"What ideas can you think of to try and resolve this dilemma?"

"How full are your five life domains with the resources you need to complete your journey?"(pull out your WLR sheet and review it with client.)

# WEIGHING THE PROS AND CONS

"What are the benefits or disadvantages of sticking to your recovery plan?"

"Where are these feeling you expressed taking you?"

"Identify for us the three best alternatives to..."

"Let's look at the pros and cons of each of the three alternatives and see which one works best."

"What's the best that could happen if...?"

"What's the worst that could happen if...?"

QUESTIONS THAT ILLICIT OPTIONS

"What could you begin doing about this today?"

"What are other courses of action you could take…?"

"Give me three options for how you could solve this challenge?"

"Out of these three options, what else could you do?"

"Which options look the most doable (list them)"

"What have you seen others do that might work for you?"

"What other resources could you tap into that…?"

"Let's try something radical here. What if the obstacles were removed, what would you do then?"

DECISION-MAKING QUESTIONS

"What do you plan to do next?"

"What are you willing to do to resolve this problem?"

"What step would you like to take to keep moving forward?"

"What is holding you back from making a decision?"

"What is the worst that can happen if you risk and try...?"

"What are some steps you have already taken to...?"

"What steps will you take to put your solution into action?"

"Are you willing to write that into your recovery plan?"

"What are the signs that point toward your being ready?"

Empowering Questions

"Which steps did you take this week to get you closer to your goal?"

"How will you handle challenges like this in the future?"

(response)"All right...way to go...that's what we're talking about."

"Which option are you ready to pursue?"

"Let's turn that into an "action" step: what will happen and by when?"

"On a scale of one to ten, how likely is it that___ will happen? How could you move that from a ___ to a ten?"

"You mentioned (three) alternatives. Which one do you feel comfortable pursuing?"

"What proof will you look for to indicate your option is succeeding?"

"Are you ready for the next assignment." (give high five or some kind of sincere praise)

PRESS ON!

I close this session with a reminder to work the suggestions outlined herein. For every addiction survivor, sobriety is a minute by minute choice. Therefore, authenticity is the key to a coaching relationship. If it's something you don't have, then it's something you will have to cultivate. You are now a co-investigator and a life strategist. While you are with us, relax, do your best, have fun, model hope, and keep a positive attitude. Your goal now is to *wander* alongside your clients in the present toward options and solution that may lie in the future; rather than marching them toward what you think are solutions. You will be guiding people through some life-changing experiences, who with your help will cause them to want adopt a more balanced life. We welcome you to Recovery Coaching Academy.

Louis Gonzales, *M.S., Ph.D., CMLC*

ENDORSEMENTS

Many people describe *Starting Point Academy's* training experience as a turning point in both their professional and personal lives. Recovery Coach Academy may rank among the most comprehensive and effective training that you have ever experienced. Here's what people say:

"This was a major turning point in both my personal and professional life."
  (J. Buerkle, Social Worker, Canoga Park, Ca.)

"I have found new ways to help people to move forward in their recovery."
  (H.A.J. Alcoholic Anonymous, Sponsor)

"Dr. Lou is the Jedi Master of recovery coaching."
(Franklin Scott, District Attorney)

"Since I am a half world away I feel blessed to have learned the way Dr. Lou communicated the essence of recovery and it's benefits. His extremely well-developed materials were presented in such a practical, yet professional way. Thank you Dr. Lou!"
(Leigh-Ann Brierley, Educator; Johannesburg, South Africa)

"Thank you for kick-starting my new career."
(M.G. Franklin, Chicago IL. Career Coach)

TRAIN TO BECOME A PROFESSIONAL
RECOVERY COACH

Starting Point offers distance learning for our Recovery Coach Certification course. Our training is crafted from *evidence-based practices* of leading industry professionals and offers participants authoritative resources from coaches and addiction professionals who are using these methods daily to help boost Recovery Capital. Recovery coaching is a great way of bridging the gap between the end of treatment and functioning at full capacity once again.

- Starting Point recovery coaches provide workable solutions and peer support to youths and adults committed to a path of long-term sobriety.

- Our coaches provide assistance with: maintaining sobriety, transforming one's life, managing anger, and building a successful business online.

- Course pricing ($575) is affordable because we have eliminated travel and hotel expenses for students.

- You will receive 30 hours equivalency: live training, 200 pg. workbook,reading materials, exercises, and after-training consultation. Your training will be either individual format on line from the comfort of your home or office via an invitation to a large group training.

Visit: www.startingpointacademy.com or call (612) 483-7676.

SOURCES AND INSPIRATION

I would like to thank those whose works inspired me throughout this project and who not only contributed thoughts, theories and notions, but gave their kind permission to use excerpts from their works. They include: Staff members at Al-Anon Family Group Headquarters, Alcoholics Anonymous, New Beginnings at Waverly, Partnership for a Drug-Free America, Relate Counseling Center of Minnesota, and, of course, Pastor John Randall of the Calvary Chapel in San Juan Capistrano.

I am indebted to every young man and woman who has ever taken a brief detour in life through addictive behaviors and who has broken through to the other side. They are the ones living their lives as inspiring examples of the power of *rational recovery*. It is these brave souls who have given me insights and allowed me the privilege of being their voice of reason. Through them, I have also learned a great deal about myself.

I would also like to acknowledge the contributions of various organizations in the addiction recovery field and the following writers whose excerpts I respectively borrowed to drive home key points:

- *The Purpose Driven Life*: *What On Earth Am I Here For.* Rick Warren.
- *Spiritual Bankruptcy parts 1,2.* Dr. Steve Frisch.
- *The Power of Now:* Eckhart Tolle
- *The Language of Letting Go:* Melodie Beattie

- *Developing a Relapse Prevention Plan.* Terrance Gorski;
- CENAPS.
- *Motivational Enhancement Therapy with Drug Abusers.* William R. Miller, Ph.D.
- *Twelve Things to Do When Booze and Drugs are Gone.* Edgar Allen Ph.D.
- *Starting Recovery with Relapse Prevention.* Terence T. Gorski
- *The Dance of Wounded Souls.* Robert Burney
- *Now That You're Sober.* Earnie Larsen with Carol Larsen Hegarty.

> If I missed anyone, please contact me at the web email listed in the front cover.
>
> Ciao!

www.ingramcontent.com/pod-product-compliance
Lightning Source LLC
Chambersburg PA
CBHW070053260726
48658CB00002B/873